How to Make a Million Dollars Trading Options:

Secrets from a Professional Trader

Publishers Note: This was anonymously emailed to us from a successful trader who became disgruntled with Wall Street but didn't want his name publicly disclosed.

How to Make a Million Dollars Trading Options:

Secrets from a Professional Trader

Copyright © 2017, Lancaster Chatham Publishing

Anonymous Email: I'm a successful options trader. I work at (redacted) and I am (redacted) I can't talk about my total profits due to my confidentiality clauses in my contract, but suffice it to say I have made a lot of money trading for my clients. I see retail investors like you getting ripped off every day, and I would like to change that. The primary reasons that people lose money when trading options is that they don't know how to value assets (this gets worse the more complex the assets are), and their expenses are too high. I estimate that the public loses over a billion dollars annually attempting to trade options.

Understand The (Actual) Basics Of Options

When we use options:

1. **When I want big time leverage on a stock moving to the upside– I buy call options.**
2. **When I want to take advantage of heightened volatility in the market or make a bet on what price a stock will trade at expiration–I sell net credit spreads, almost always put spreads.**

Almost every other thing that you can do in the options market is designed by market makers to transfer your money into their pocket over time.

There are a million strategies you can use to try to make money in options. I think 95 percent of them are garbage. I will break down the expected returns of each option strategy later.

Options, simply put, are the right to buy or sell a stock. The right to buy is called a call option, and the right to sell is called a put option. The buyer pays an upfront premium in exchange for this right, and if the stock doesn't move the way they expect, they aren't forced to do anything, which is why they are called "options". All stock options have specified prices where you are permitted to buy or sell the stock; this is called the **strike price**. You have the choice of buying options to buy the stock below the current trading price- "in the money," at the current price-"at the money," or above the current price-"out of the money". The further out of the money the option is, the riskier the bet. Also, options are only good for so long, meaning they expire. The expiration date for equity options in the United States was traditionally after the market close on the third Friday of the month, but nowadays, the exchanges offer options that expire every single Friday. This is the **expiration date** you see when you look up options on your online brokerage. Also, American call and put options trade in 100 share contracts, so if you buy one call option, it gives you the right to 100 shares. If you buy 20, that's 2000 shares. However, the quote you see on your online brokerage account is per share, so remember to multiply by 100!

People who buy options do so because they get an enormous amount of leverage for the money, *meaning if the stock moves a little, they make a lot of money.* People who sell options do so to collect the premiums. One of the biggest groups of options sellers are retired people who sell options on stocks they own to bring in steady income. Banks and stock trading firms sell a lot of options too, but typically use complex hedging techniques to ensure they make a profit no matter which way the market moves. My research indicates that sellers have a systematic advantage over buyers, but options sellers tend to make steadier profits punctuated by quick drawdowns, while options buyers tend to see more in the way of feast or famine returns.

However, call options have high, positive returns, and are deadly in the hands of a skilled trader. I will break down the theory and show the advantages and disadvantages of each group later.

How do you trade options? You trade options the same way you trade stocks, go to your online brokerage account and usually next to where you input orders for stocks, you can input orders for options. You do usually need to fill out a form or two acknowledging the risks of trading options before you begin, but the process to get in to trading options is not that difficult. If you are a first time options trader, you usually get by default what is called a level 2 approval to buy calls and puts, and sell calls covered by stock positions (level 1). Level 3 approval is not too hard to get either, and it allows you to sell options, provided you have enough cash to cover the maximum loss or do a credit spread to hedge the risk.

If you believe that Apple is going to go higher and AAPL is trading for 135 dollars a share, you can buy a call option giving you the right to buy AAPL at 135 for 30 days. In this example, let's say your premium is 2 dollars per share and you buy 25 contracts. If AAPL rallies to 140, you can exercise the option to buy for 135 a share, and immediately sell for 140. Don't worry about not having the money to exercise an option; your broker will do it for you even if you don't have the money to buy the stock outright. Your profit in this case would be 3 dollars per share multiplied by the 2500 shares in the contract, pocketing you a cool 7500 dollars on a less than 5 percent move in the stock over a month. You just tripled your money! The benefit to buying call options on a stock is that your gain is theoretically unlimited. For example, if by some freak accident AAPL skyrockets to 150 per share, you wind up pocketing 32,500 dollars on your trade, and this happens often enough that you hear about it from other traders, usually when they put pictures of their new BMWs on Facebook. However, if AAPL sinks to 130, or even holds steady at 135, you lose your entire investment of 2500 dollars. However, one of the keys to success trading options is to not always hold them until the end of their expiration, as you will see in a little while. That way, if the stock doesn't move when you think it is going to, you can sell your option and get a good chunk of your money back if you don't wait until the expiration date. *Options are like milk; they're best for your health when they're not about to expire.* An important thing to note about options is that you can sell them at any time; you don't need to wait until the expiration to exercise them. *In fact, you should never exercise an option when you can sell instead.* There are theoretically times when you should exercise instead of selling, it usually happens with deep in the money options around dividend payout dates and stocks with wide bid/ask spreads on their options. In practice, the large number of arbitrageurs trading with complex software means that I have never been in a situation over my thousands of trades where I would have been better off by exercising. That situation will never happen in AAPL, although it might happen on a small stock with thinly traded options. You will find this to be true for you also. For example, if AAPL rallies to 137 in the first week, the option should be worth 3 dollars and change, but if you exercise, you lose the extra premium.

Anyway, you trade options the same way you trade stocks, through your online broker order entry screen, the only difference is that options have some different characteristics. These characteristics are known as the "Greeks". Each Greek can be derived with some not so simple math from the Black Scholes equation. No worries though, if you use an online brokerage that supports options trading, the computer will do the math for you to spit out the Greeks. There are 5 major Greeks, I tend to pay attention to 3 of them in my trading. The other two are Vega and Rho, give the terms a Google if you are interested, they apply more to strategies I don't employ. The first Greek is called Delta. *Delta is just the amount that the option goes up in value if the stock goes up a dollar per share.* Delta is expressed as a number from 0 to 1. Options that are really far in the money are going to have Deltas close to 1, meaning that if the stock moves up a dollar, so do the options. Options that are at the money will always have a Delta of roughly 0.5, meaning they go up about 50 cents for every dollar the stock moves. Options that are out of the money have Deltas closer to zero, because the stock has to move a long way for them to have any value. For example, if you buy 145 strike calls in AAPL when it is trading for 135, you might only get a 10 cent increase in the value of your options until it gets closer to the money. Note that Delta changes as the stock moves up and down. An option that is out of the money can become in the money if the stock moves up sharply, making the buyer of the option a lot of money in the process. *In the real world, Traders use Delta as a proxy for the probability that the stock will be at or above the strike price when the option expires.*

When the Delta changes on a stock due to the options going further in the money or further out of the money, this change is expressed as Gamma. Gamma is simply the rate that Delta changes. So, if the stock goes up a dollar per share, the delta will increase. Gamma is also measured as a decimal from 0 to 1. For normal trading, all you need to know is that the Delta will increase when the stock goes up, and will decrease if the stock goes down.

The third, and most important Greek, in my opinion, is Theta. In exchange for unlimited rewards on the upside of a stock, call buyers have to pay a premium to be able to buy the stock at a fixed price for a period of time. There are two parts to the value of an option, time premium, and intrinsic value. Time premium shrinks nearly every day, and at the end of the option, all that is left is the intrinsic value, meaning the option is in the money and the option has value due to the ability to sell or exercise for a profit. If the option is not in the money at the expiration, it has no intrinsic value. The time premium will also be valued at zero at expiration, so the option is *worthless*. Every day the stock doesn't go up, the value of the option suffers from **time decay**, which is expressed as Theta. Theta is written as a decimal and is the amount that the time premium of option will decay per day, regardless of whether the stock goes up or down. Theta works 24/7 to erode the value of call options. It works kind of like the event horizon of a black hole. One thing I notice from my trading is that time decay (Theta) seems to happen in chunks. If the stock holds steady for the day and the option isn't close to expiration, sometimes the option won't drop at all, but if the stock sells off the next day, the options will get absolutely crushed and lose even more time premium than you would expect. Theta can be your worst enemy or your best friend; it just depends on how you set up your strategies. If you sell options, you will be toasting to Theta all the time, and if you buy them, you will curse Theta on a daily basis.

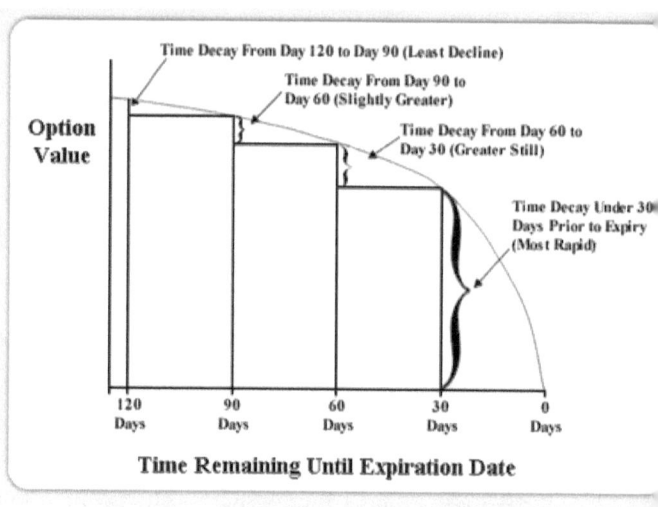

The most time decay in the life of an option occurs in the last month of its existence before expiration. Notice what happens about a week out, the value of the option goes straight down like the option is falling into a black hole. This is where I like to sell out of the money put options, but so I don't want to risk losing massive amounts of money, I hedge the puts I sell with a put a ways further out of the money so I know the maximum loss I can sustain. This is important to do because of the black swan risk that is present in the market at all times, when selling puts, you are only one "flash crash" away from bankruptcy. I'm sure a few traders were bankrupted back in 2010 when the infamous "flash crash" scrubbed a trillion dollars in US market value in 36 minutes. So, limit your risk when you sell puts, just like insurance companies buy reinsurance, you should buy cheap puts so you can quantify your maximum loss but still take advantage of the positive expected value of your trade. The beauty of trading put spreads is that options get more expensive the more stocks go down, due to increased volatility, puts included. *This gives you an opportunity to make some cash every time the market has a decent correction.* If the market falls 10 percent, it doesn't become riskier in my opinion, I think it becomes less risky. I think you can make some nice cash by selling "insurance" by selling puts into market corrections, and covering your ass by buying a much further out of the money put. When you do this, it's called a credit spread, because you get cash deposited into your account when you make the trade, and when the option expires out of the money, you pocket 100 percent, free and clear.

I'm not a Nobel prize winning mathematician by any means, but I think it would stand to reason that you are better off holding options that have a month or two left to go if you want to be buying them, and if you want to sell options, you are better off taking advantage of that exponential rate of decline at the end of the graph by selling options with less than a month out. It is somewhat riskier to sell options closer to expiration, and it does decrease your upside to pay more premiums to buy a call option with a couple months to live, but that's my preferred way of trading options. I do not believe that the options market is fully efficient. I will explain why in a little while, and you are welcome to agree or disagree with me.

Understand Volatility and

Put/Call Parity

The Greeks are the characteristics of how options move in relation to the stock, but how are they determined? Why is an option for AAPL at 135 worth 2 dollars a share for a month? Options get their value from volatility. Next to the Greeks on any options quote you see on your online brokerage is a number for **implied volatility.** Options are valued based on the underlying volatility of the stock, which is quoted as an annualized standard deviation. In plain English, the implied volatility is how much the market expects the stock to move over the next year, based on the price of the option. Again, you don't need to know advanced calculus to derive the implied volatility number; your computer will do it for you. You can readily compare the implied volatility with the **historical volatility** of the same stock, which is usually calculated as the volatility of the stock over the past 30 days. The historical volatility isn't always on the same screen, most brokers have a way to find the historical volatility, you just have to search around sometimes, and even if your broker doesn't have it, there are online services you can use. If you want to trade options seriously, you need this data. Etrade and Interactive Brokers both have the historical volatility as an option in their stock charts.

The thing is, implied volatility and historical volatility are usually different numbers. This can occur for a variety of reasons, such as an upcoming earnings announcement, a more volatile market, or bias on the part of traders. The interesting thing I have found in my research is that traders are consistently biased in their view of implied volatility. *In fact, over long periods of time, the average implied volatility is around 19 percent, whereas the average realized volatility of the options is only about 16 percent.* (Eraker, 2007, NYU Stern School of Business) This translates into large profits for sellers of options, especially put options, as you will see in a little while. So, if traders are consistently overvaluing options, we can systematically take advantage of their bias. Furthering this advantage is the fact that stocks tend to go up over time, favoring call buyers and put sellers. Puts and calls can't reflect the return of the underlying stock, because they are forced to trade at parity by arbitrage. This is called put/call parity.

The equation for this, in its simplest form, is that **Stock=Call-Put.** You can replicate a stock position of 100 shares, for example, by buying an at the money call, and selling a put, meaning you take the risk all the way to zero on the 100 shares stock, and you have unlimited upside on the 100 shares, and your options premiums will cancel each other out. If they didn't you could make free money by arbitrage, synthetically creating puts, calls or stock from buying and selling the other two. No matter how you rearrange this algebraically, it remains true. So if you want a call, it is the same thing as owning stock and buying a put to protect your downside. If you want a put, you need minus stock (short selling), and to buy a call. This may be difficult to do if you are a retail trader, but to Wall Street traders with 8 and 9 figure lines of credit, it could not be easier to synthetically arbitrage stocks and options. Why is this important that stocks and puts have to trade at parity? The reason why this is important is that the expected return for a put and a call are not the same, even if they are forced to trade at parity by arbitrage. The only factor that affects how puts and calls are valued is the volatility of the underlying stock, not the expected return. The expected return of stocks is positive, meaning put buyers collectively lose boatloads of cash, and call buyers collectively make boatloads of cash. It doesn't sound like it should be this simple, but it really is. *Calls really are just highly leveraged positions in appreciating assets. Puts, on the other hand, are insurance.* Insurance is meant to protect your assets against loss, not make you a profit. Therefore, institutional investors sometimes sell puts to protect their large stock positions from downside. Note that this doesn't kill their returns completely, just reduces their risk in exchange for peace of mind. The people who sell them insurance, on the other hand, make a profit on average, and a very good one if they control risk properly. Retail investors make mistakes when they trade options, focusing too much on buying puts, buying calls that are too far out of the money, and timing their trades poorly.

Know the Expected Value

of Options Contracts

The key to making money trading is being able to value the expected return of an asset better than the suckers you trade against, and if you do that, you make money. I said before that the way I like to trade options is to either use long call options as a proxy for stock, or use net credit spreads as to play volatility. But how do you select expirations, strikes, etc? Expiration is easy to select, just pick an expiration that gives you a little more time than you think you need, with a minimum of a couple weeks to go if you are buying, and a couple weeks or less if you are selling. Strike prices, on the other hand, is a little complicated, so we need to delve a little into options pricing theory to fully understand it. As I discussed in the put/call parity section, call options are basically a substitute for long stock, except with limited downside. **What I am going to prove to you is that the higher your strike price is, the higher your expected return is, and the higher your risk is also.** This holds true all the way until the option is at the money, out of the money options are valued a little differently because a lot of people buy them as lottery tickets. So remember that **Stock=Call-Put?** If the strike equals zero, then you can't sell a put, since the right to sell a stock for zero is worthless. Therefore, stock is a call option with a strike price of zero. Your risk of loss is limited to your total investment, since stocks can't trade for negative amounts. Now, on AAPL, there are strikes all the way from 45 dollars per share in the current month all the way to 200 dollars a share. I went through the options chains to see the values for each option, and I had to go to the 130 strike before I found any options with a delta less than 99 cents per dollar. Time premium isn't really coming into play here at all until you hit the 125 strike. AAPL trades at about 136 at the time of writing this.

For example, on the 50-dollar strike, you are paying 86 dollars to per share to control a stock that is worth 136 dollars. You are getting some nice leverage for less than a 1 percent implied interest rate! On the 100-dollar strike, you pay about 36 dollars to control a 136-dollar stock, giving you roughly 4-1 leverage. The Delta is still 99.7, so you really are getting this leverage. On the 125 strike, you get a delta of around 97, and you have 13-1 leverage on the stock. Want to get the maximum bang for your buck on a 1-dollar move in the stock? In my experience, you get the most bang for your buck by buying the strike nearest to the stock price. The 135 strike here gives you about 40 to 1 leverage on AAPL. Calculate your **Delta** by multiplying the number of shares you get in your contract by the quoted Delta. Then divide by how much this cost you to get your **leverage** on the stock. You will theoretically make more money from out of the money options for large stock moves, but my research indicates that out of the money call options tend to be overvalued and have flat or negative expected returns. There are a lot of studies that have been done on the expected returns of options, which get some contradictory results, but I found one to be more helpful than the others. The study, done by two gentlemen named Coval and Shumway at the University of Michigan Business School found that call option returns increase as you go higher in the strike price, and that at the money calls return roughly a positive 2.5 percent per week on average. They also noted that while the absolute returns on call options are impressive (10-12 percent per month, on average), and over 100 percent per year, the risk adjusted returns kind of suck. They thought that for the risk, calls should return about 4 percent per week. This makes sense though, because of the incredible amount of leverage that call options give you trading stocks. How does this help you make money? It tells you 2 things.

1. Blindly buying call options isn't a good idea for the amount of risk that you take. Call options that are in the money or at the money do better than those that are out of the money.

2. Call options have huge returns, and equally huge risk.

By the way, here's what they found the returns were for buying puts. The average put return per week? Minus 6-7 percent!! Buying puts to place concentrated bets against stocks doesn't sound that dumb, but when you look at the numbers, you have a colossal wealth transfer happening on a daily basis due to people buying puts. Imagine if your car insurance cost 7 percent of your car's value per week. You would go bankrupt. Coval and Shumway point out that many people who buy puts do so to protect their long stock positions, but I personally suspect that there are a few townhouses in Manhattan paid for by retail traders buy puts on companies they hate. In this same vein, strategies like straddles are very poor investments. Inside the mind of an amateur trader "I don't know which way Apple will move after earnings, but I think it will move a lot," so I will buy both calls and puts. WRONG. You wouldn't go on a gambling spree before you go buy personal umbrella insurance, so don't buy puts and calls at the same time either. You can't afford to ignore the statistics of the markets if you want to be rich.

Call options, despite not having the best risk adjusted returns, are a deadly tool in the hands of a good trader. Since call option values are connected with the value of the underlying stock, anyone who can make good money trading stocks can make great money trading options.

How to Size Your Trades: John Kelly vs. John Daly

One of the biggest questions in trading is how much capital to bet on each trade. There are a variety of methods, and I will give them each a grade based on how well I think they work.

The John Daly Method- **Grade–F** Most traders are gunslingers. They size their trades based on their convictions, and swing for the fences far too often. Their trading style reminds me of former professional golfer John Daly. I love John Daly's game, the man was very long off the tee, but I probably wouldn't give him my money to manage. Don't be the kind of trader who swings for the fences every time, betting 30-50 percent of your capital on each penny stock or options trade. If you swing for the fences every time, you end up risking losing all of your money. Having no plan is not having a trading plan.

The Martingale- **Grade–F** If you have ever been to a casino, you have seen someone do the Martingale. Basically, how the martingale works is every time you lose a bet (trade), you double the size of your bet (trade) until you make your money back. A martingale trader usually starts with betting like 5,000 per trade on a 100,000 dollar account and doubling down every time they lose. 95 percent of the time, it works and they run up your account balance to a little higher than you started, at which point the martingale trader usually withdraws the profit and goes on a spending spree. "What are the odds of losing 7 times in a row," they usually declare. They always end up broke, because some time in the course of their life, they do indeed lose 7 in a row or 8 in a row or whatever it takes to bankrupt them.

Fixed Amount- **Grade D+** A lot of traders like to bet a fixed amount on each trade, for example if they have a 50,000 dollar trading account, they bet a flat 5,000 on every trade. While not as exaggerated as the martingale, fixed amount betting runs into some of the same problems as the martingale, namely that it doesn't increase exposure when times are going well and decrease it when the account is vulnerable from drawdowns.

Fixed Fractional- **Grade C+** Fixed fractional traders will put, for example, 10 percent of their available capital in each trade, giving them protection from drawdowns and allowing them to benefit from rising markets by placing progressively more capital at play. The reason why this doesn't get an A is not all trading strategies are created equal, and traders can underbet on good strategies and overbet on bad strategies.

Full Kelly Criterion- **Grade A–** John Kelly was an engineer at AT&T in the 1950s who contributed to the field of advantage gambling and trading with his invention of the Kelly Criterion. The Kelly Criterion says to bet an amount of your capital equal to the positive expected value of the trade. For example, at the money call options have a positive expected value of 9 percent over a month, so the optimal amount of your capital to play at the money call options with is 9 percent or less. Note that the expected value of put options and far out of the money is actually negative, so the Kelly Criterion dictates that you should allocate zero dollars to them. Additionally, when using the Kelly Criterion to size trades, you can keep the rest of the money in a liquid mix of ETFs in an allocation like 85 percent bonds and 15 percent stocks, giving you an annual return averaging over 20 percent. You can make a living trading like that! The elegant part of the mathematics of the Kelly Criterion is that

Kelly maximizes the logarithmic growth of your cash. Bet any more, and your capital grows less fast. Bet any less, and you leave some money on the table.

Play With the House's Money- **Grade A+** The Kelly Criterion (Fractional)- The best way to trade is to build on my earlier point about keeping the other 90 percent of your capital invested in less risky bets. One key point of modern portfolio theory is that you can invest in multiple risky assets, and collectively they are safer than any one individual bet. You don't have to bet the whole 9 percent on call options per month, in fact, you can bet less and your returns decrease more slowly than your risk decreases. To trade properly, set up two accounts, one for long-term investments, and one for trading. Put all your current money into a long-term investment account, but take the dividends and after tax capital gains and put them in your trading account. When you make new cash contributions to your account, do 70 percent into your long-term investment account, and put 30 percent into your trading account. This way, you are always playing with the house's money. Let the returns of your trading strategies drive your bet size, not the other way around! Do this, and you put yourself on the path to raking in the cash.

Where to Find Trading

Ideas

1. The 52-week high list. I am always a fan of trading on momentum. Research shows that stocks at their 52 week highs tend to continue to go up. These are the Amazons, Googles and Apples of the world, and great companies tend to find themselves perpetually at the 52 week high. This tends to work best for stocks over 100 dollars a share–share prices send an important signal about the underlying company. How does a company trade for 900 dollars a

share, like Amazon does? The do it by being damn successful! Stocks end up at 5 dollars a share because they lose money. Stocks end up in the triple digits because they make money. Plain and simple.

2. Short Selling firms. I'm not really a fan of shorting stocks, I don't think it tends to be profitable, but there are research firms that publish about stocks they think are overvalued or straight up fraudulent. The most notable of these firms is Citron Research. I've been on both sides of Citron's calls, and they have made me a lot of money when I have been on their side and lost me money when they called against me. You don't have to trade in the same direction as

Citron or any other notable short selling firms, but you should understand that they move the market. Follow them on twitter, and they'll send you calls in real time.

3. StockTwits. Ever hung out at a craps table? Stocktwits is the online trading version of a craps table. Go to front page of Stocktwits and they have a section for trending stocks. These are the most talked about, and therefore traded stocks of the day. See what other people are saying, form your own opinion, and fire away. You already know that long options are the way to go, so when you see stocks moving up on stocktwits to a lot of chatter, buy them, sell them a few hours later, and profit.

Why Most Options Traders Lose Money

Trading is a business. If you go long stocks or their derivatives, you should make money over time. This is the market rewarding you for taking risk (*beta*). If you beat other traders over time, this adds an additional component to your profit (*alpha*). Your gross profit is equal to your alpha plus your beta. That is your gross profit. Your expenses are your commissions, fees, bid/ask spreads, and margin interest. The dirty little secret about trading is that most traders make money before expenses, and lose money after expenses. This is a business, not a game. Here's what you can do about each expense.

- Commissions- Use Robin Hood or Interactive Brokers. As of writing this, I don't think you can do options on Robin

Hood, but they are free for stocks. Interactive Brokers is 1 dollar per trade, vs Etrade which charges 6.95. By not using a retail oriented broker like Etrade or Scottrade you cut your commission cost 85 plus percent. Do you want to make money or lose money? Pay attention to your damn expenses! 80 percent of retail traders are at firms that charge over 5 dollars in commission. Wall Street nibbles away at your cash, getting rich off you and transferring your money into their pocket, 7 bucks at a time.

- Fees- This mainly applies to longer term investors who pay people to manage their money for them. If you are paying any fees, you need to be able to justify them, just like if you were running a business.

- Bid/Ask spreads- Do you have 1 million dollars in stock you need to take liquidity for to sell? If not, why are you using market orders? This is a Wall Street scam. In business, the person who makes the offer typically gets a better price. Case in point, car dealers offer cars for sale, and buy them cheap at auction. They always name their price. Who doesn't name their price? Dumb consumers who want a brand new car and don't like negotiating. Business requires you to negotiate, use limit orders for your inventory.

- Margin Interest- If you are paying 9 plus percent to borrow stocks when Interactive

Brokers charges 2 percent, you are an idiot. That's fine though, there is still time to switch to a broker that charges a better rate for margin. Etrade charges like 10 percent on margin, that's what the expected return of most stocks is. So the customer takes 100 percent of the risk, and Etrade gets 10 percent, risk free... Genius for Etrade, horribly stupid for anyone who borrows from them.

Bonus Tips on Trading

- When you set limit orders to buy or sell, set them at random prices, not at round numbers. For example, set your order for

99.98 instead of 100, because lots of institutional traders are lazy and call in round numbers to their brokers.
- Large Bid/ Ask spreads can either represent opportunity or trouble for options traders. You don't want to trade contracts that aren't liquid, but if, for example, the bid is for 0.90 and the ask is for 1.05 on an option, I would try to buy for 0.90 and sell for 1.05. You just have to be patient and move the limit around if it doesn't work in the first 20 minutes or so. Volatility can be your friend as much as your enemy, Benjamin Graham and Warren Buffett would agree.
- Patience is key, every 9-12 months you typically see a 9-10 percent pullback in

stocks. Corrections are guaranteed to happen, don't stress out of the market is too calm. Go play golf instead or take time off to travel if the market is slow. The market as a whole tends to be really slow from mid July to mid August, that is an excellent time of year to take a break from trading for you also. If half of Wall Street is frolicking in the Hamptons, you should do something similar. Emulate the successful, trading isn't the kind of job where you make money for showing up every day. It is more important to not be wrong than to be right.

- For your first trade of the quarter or your first trade with a new deposit, do something high percentage to put a win on the board. Selling out of the money weekly puts works well for this. It is so much easier to make money with a positive attitude and nothing inspires a positive attitude like playing with the house's money.

The public loses billions trading options, and the only people who know why won't tell the public. *Approach trading like a business and you are well on your way to making money. Approach it like entertainment, and you will get what you pay for.* Expected value is everything, do the math and follow the money. Nothing can make you more money than smart speculation, and sometimes all it takes is a couple good options trades in a row. That's what worked for me.

Until Next Time,

Cameron Lancaster

www.ingramcontent.com/pod-product-compliance
Lightning Source LLC
Chambersburg PA
CBHW020708180526
45163CB00008B/2997